BALDWIN'S CATHOLIC GEESE

Keith Hutson has written for *Coronation Street* and for many well-known comedians. His award-winning poetry has been widely-published both in the UK and internationally. He plays to packed houses and was a 2018 Laureate's Choice poet. He is a member of the *Poetry Salzburg* editorial board and delivers poetry and performance workshops in schools for the Prince's Trust.

A Mancunian by birth, Keith now lives in Halifax, West Yorkshire, where he is Poet-in-Residence at the Square Chapel Theatre. He has an MA (Poetry) from Manchester Metropolitan University. His pamphlets, *Routines* (Poetry Salzburg, 2016) and *Troupers* (Smith|Doorstop, 2018), were followed by his first book-length collection, *Baldwin's Catholic Geese*, from Bloodaxe in 2019.

KEITH HUTSON

Baldwin's Catholic Geese

For Claudia,
with love &
best wishes,
Keith

BLOODAXE BOOKS

ISBN: 978 1 78037 455 0

First published 2019 by
Bloodaxe Books Ltd,
Eastburn,
South Park,
Hexham,
Northumberland NE46 1BS.

www.bloodaxebooks.com
For further information about Bloodaxe titles
please visit our website and join our mailing list
or write to the above address for a catalogue

Cover design: Neil Astley & Pamela Robertson-Pearce.

Printed in Great Britain by Bell & Bain Limited, Glasgow, Scotland, on
acid-free paper sourced from mills with FSC chain of custody certification.

for Robert and Adele

and, of course, Fiona

ACKNOWLEDGEMENTS

Acknowledgements are due to: *Bare Fiction, The Fenland Reed, The Fortnightly Review, The Friend, Grey Suit Poetry, The High Window, The Interpreter's House, London Grip, Magma, The Manhattan Review, The North, Poetry Salzburg Review, Prole, Spilling Cocoa Over Martin Amis, Stand* and *Vanguard Anthology 2.*

Some of these poems, or earlier versions, appeared in two pamphlets, *Routines* (Poetry Salzburg, 2016) and *Troupers* (Smith | Doorstop, Laureate's Choice, 2018)

'Caretaker' was longlisted in the 2018 National Poetry Competition judged by Hannah Lowe and Andrew McMillan. 'The Call of the Wild' was shortlisted in the 2017 Cornwall Contemporary Poetry Competiton judged by Alison Brackenbury. 'Civic Theatre' won 3rd place in the 2015 Poetry Business Yorkshire Prize judged by Billy Collins. 'Coming On Strong' was Commended in the 2016 York Literature Festival Competition judged by Carole Bromley. 'I'm Here All Week' was shortlisted for the 2017 Wordsworth Trust Prize judged by Mimi Khalvati and Ian Duhig. 'Tiddly Om Pom Pom' won 2nd place in the 2016 Manchester Metropolitan University Sonnet Competition judged by Carol Ann Duffy. 'Vera' was Commended in the 2016 Mclellan Prize judged by David Constantine. The quartet of 'No Contest', 'The Fish Fryer', 'Heart' and 'Coming On Strong' was Highly Commended in the 2016 RNCM/MMU Rosamond Prize, a poet/composer musical collaboration judged by Michael Symmons Roberts. 'Bad Impresario' was Highly Commended in the 2017 Rosamond Prize.

Many thanks to David Constantine, Ian Duhig, Clare Shaw.

Special thanks to Neil Astley, Michael Symmons Roberts, and Ann and Peter Sansom.

Particular thanks to Carol Ann Duffy for all her encouragement and support.

CONTENTS

Pray temper your hilarity
with a modicum of restraint

GEORGE ROBEY 1869-1954

The Opener

Do not book a buffoon. People can't cope,
still finding seats and folding coats, heavy
with home: they'll barrack or shut down.

Avoid, therefore, all turns with titles
like *The Elongated Chump*,
Breezy Comedienne or *Just Let Loose!*

See every house, before it settles,
as a beast not fully backed into its cage.
Don't spook the bugger with a premature attack

from *Don's Inebriated Dart-Blowers*; a dose
of *Madame Zanza*, *Boneless in the Buff*
unless she's very, very still.

Aim for warmth, but not *The Beneditti Three:*
Musicians in Fifty Positions –
they generate too much too soon,

while *Harry Norton The Human Hydrant*
would fill the gents before the interval.
Regurgitators always block the ladies up.

Never let *fartistes* on till the end;
paper-tearers, shadowgraphists,
omnivores and *infant-mimics*, not even then.

Play safe, get someone big and jovial
but suitably restrained – unless that's how
they've been described by the police.

Juvenile

i.m. Georgie Doonan 1897-1973

In time to a drumbeat, Georgie Doonan
kicked his own backside. Some critics called it
nothing but self-injury with rhythm.
A newspaper dismissed the act as fit
only for idiots with no command
over their sense of wonder, and went on
to call for Tom Platt and His Talking Pond,
no less, to *come back, all is forgiven!*

So why, when Georgie booted his behind,
did those who knew no better split their sides?
He must have made an impact deeper down.
And I know I'd have laughed, which won't surprise
you if you've ever run on joy alone,
heels bouncing bum-high; if that's what you've known.

Coming On Strong

i.m. Joan Rhodes 1921-2010

Three and in the workhouse, ten when you ran,
missing till twenty then, as lean as luck,
in fishnets at the fair, you tore a phone book
up, bent iron bars, broke nails, took four men

on at tug-of-war and won, which led to
lifting Bob Hope while Marlene Dietrich
loved a woman tough enough to keep
refusing King Farouk, who wanted you

to wreck his best four-poster bed with him
still in it. Joan, I've seen your photograph,
fab in a basque and tan, that cast-iron bath
held high, before you disappeared again,

found in a care home where, I understand,
greeting the manager, you broke his hand.

Revival

Like the funniest of men, he had that look:
bad health crossed with indestructibility.
Fans would slap and cuddle him.

It takes a certain type of body to appear,
night after night, as if a gang's manhandled
it into a dinner suit; face folded
like a heart attack was homing in.

It was. But he'd soaked several up already;
recovered with a crack:
Treading boards is my best exercise!

After the last, wrapped in an overcoat
on Blackpool prom, he'd seemed robust enough,
just pale. And people like him, whose fathers

died in harness, whose mothers bore silent,
determined lives, they never bow out barely used.
One way or another they sweat buckets,
under stress, and make that state hilarious.

That's why we wet ourselves when they collapse
at the Palladium. And why it's only right
to raise another smile, to bring them back.

The Fish Fryer

i.m. Billy Bennett 1887-1942

The secret is to get the audience
to flinch with you: imaginary hot fat
should surprise them too. A shared experience.
But ration out the twitches, make every spit
and spatter count. Your elbow action should,
however, never stop. You've got to work
that non-existent haddock, scallop, cod
till they can smell the sizzling. You'll look
a fool, standing on stage behind a range
that isn't there, but that's what they've all paid
good money for. Somehow it entertains
them – a ninny in a pinny plagued
by boiling oil. Don't try to analyse
their appetites, though. That way madness lies.

No Contest

i.m. Nervo and Knox, entwined 1919-1952

Slow-motion wrestling: painfully tense
for the participants whose audience,
however, had to cultivate patience,

a love of mission-creep eked out in sweat,
as two men coaxed one show-stopping headlock
from such a fractured tussle that the clock

became immobilised as well, or so
it seemed to those who watched half-nelsons grow,
glacial-pace, to full – and though I'm no

aficionado, this inch-by-inch
palaver gives me pause: where's the suspense
or business-sense it must have held since,

when a rival duo tried to muscle in,
Nervo and Knox rapidly battered them.

Lady Be Good

i.m. Ivy Benson 1913-1993

By God, she was – from clarinet and sax,
aged eight, in pubs, already patronised
at best for being *of the fairer sex*;
to Edna Croudman's Rhythm Girls, described
as *great, considering they're women*; to
the first female bandleader swinging through
more ridicule, a *bombshell in the Blitz*;
to placing male conductors' jobs *at risk*,
on tour with ENSA; to Berlin, VE Day,
frowned upon, although Montgomery
himself had called her up; top of the bill
at the Palladium, resented still
until, *she's past her best*, Ivy's *decline*
– really? – to Butlin's, also in its prime.

Hylda

i.m. Hylda Baker 1909-1986

Nine was the age the likes of her learnt
how to lip-read at the mill;
to flap their silent mouths in turn.

But Hylda found her voice inside this act,
talent that kept her in pink gins for years:
a *popular comedienne*, bottom of the bill.

Funny, then, to be described by Delfont
as an overnight success, *proprietress*
of Pledge's Pickle Factory on ITV.

They said that show went to her head.
Deaf to them, she changed her tipple to a lot
of crème de menthe, bought a bungalow

in Cleveleys, quilted bedroom floor to ceiling,
cocktail bar an opera box, doorbell
singing *Come Back to Sorrento*

as she warned reporters,
Don't be dazzled by the décor –
it's contemporary.

Barred from playing panto dame,
she made her men wear dresses, let them stay
on the condition they were dumb.

Her harem swelled, and neighbours,
outraged yet refined, presented a petition:
Please leave. Thank you.

This prompted the flagpole with
You haven't had the pleasure of me yet
flown every day and twice for matinees.

Spandex at seventy, that bump-and grind
with Arthur Mullard on *Top of the Pops*,
and then she died, demented,

utterly alone – unmourned
by impresarios and sisterhoods alike.
Nine was the number at her funeral.

Heart

i.m. Lottie Collins 1866-1910

Without a war, your fancy bloomers were
the only bit of France most blighters saw.
You hit the hardest halls for twenty years
non-stop; fed future cannon-fodder encores
till you dropped. This was not the can-can,
this was carnage – battalions of men,
hands up and howling as they wiped you out
for shrapnel, flung with kisses, twice a night.

How many thousand shows, soaked to the skin
in silk? How many high-kicks had you done,
before your heart stopped you unfolding from
the floor to take a bow? And how can we,
from here, salute you now? There's just one way,
with all we've got: *Ta-ra-ra Boom-de-ay!*

Glasgow Empire

Yes, it was here the gang show audience
slow-handclapped that girl guide
with laryngitis;

the Beverley Sisters flitted on
then promptly darted off again
to cries of *Christ, there's three of 'em!*

Where else would Eartha Kitt
be forced back out, Ken Dodd
having cut his act in half?

After Des O'Connor fainted
from derision, dragged to safety,
seventy ice creams were counted on his suit.

Even when empty, anger
occupied this auditorium. It bloomed,
silent and black: a storm building to break

above row upon row of folded seats,
all rigid as a nervous herd
before it bolts.

Bad Impresario

i.m. William Paul 1820-1882

William Paul, with millions to waste
on battling boredom, wondered which place
in Blighty had the least discerning taste:

could he unearth a town where utter tripe
would be considered culture at its height –
silk purses not sow's ears – night after night?

Two dozen hardened scouts were sent to scour
the land; five hundred flops auditioned for
his troupe; the ten most woeful went on tour

including long-abandoned novelties
like *Lady Clock Eye, Baldwin's Catholic Geese,*
The Human Mop, Frank and his Dancing Teeth:

from Cumbria to Cornwall no one asked
them back, except the Palace, Halifax.

Accept No Imitations

i.m. J.D. Plummer 1846-1901

Do your colleagues call you a control freak?
Fuck 'em. Abandoned on the first night
by his cast, JD played every character
himself: Dick Turpin, victims, innkeeper
and black-eyed daughter Bess, Dick's worn-out horse,
also called Bess, and black (this did cause
confusion), Tom the Ostler who betrayed them,
weeping Widow Shelley, Tyburn hangman,

and it ran for fifteen months, through Glossop,
Leeds and York, till he collapsed banging two
coconuts together at a gallop,
then went bankrupt, then insane. Worth it, though,
to show incompetents what can be done
by one who stands, delivers, falls, alone.

Family Business

I

Old Mother Riley, Arthur Lucan
in a bonnet, married a woman
half his age who turned into his daughter
every evening on stage.

But when curtains were closed,
she called on better men than him
to strip away the minor role
she played.

II

Albert Burdon dressed his son up
as his Ugly Sister.
When not preoccupied with balls,
their bond was brittle
as a crystal slipper.

III

Thank God for Jimmy Clitheroe,
four feet three inches of propriety,
who wore his cap and shorts
for over fifty years, but never dragged
his mum into the act.

The day they buried her,
he tucked into sufficient pills
to kill the boy
he could no longer bear to be.

My Old Man

i.m. Ephraim Barraclough 1853-1906

Tell him three traits, and he'd impersonate
your dad. This chip off everyone's old block
possessed, let's say, a patriarchal knack
to take a parent's essence, flesh it out
– the full Monty, Tom, Albert, Harry, Dick –
rough or benign, for better or for worse:
offspring whose hurt returned took flight in tears;
beloveds got a flash of hero back.

He didn't do his own though: *Little point*
aping a fellow if the audience don't
know him. Neither did Ephraim: *He left.*
That's that. Most of us let it go, except
a postman who arrived at the stage door,
ashes and cap in hand: *Your father, sir.*

The Call of the Wild

i.m. Percy Edwards 1908-1996

Has anybody risen from such bleakness,
a chicken in the chapel pageant,
cancelled? Then Old Mother Hubbard's
hopeful dog, Ipswich infants' panto:
Make an effort, little Edwards, said the head.

Who could predict, once broken in,
our boy would grow to be the perfect
Suffolk Punch, Black Mountain, Saddleback,
or any livestock loud and proud required?
But Percy wasn't just a walking farm,

he stopped Sir David Attenborough in his tracks:
A kookaburra? Ten miles from West Ham?
Guess who gave vent to pheasants, cock
and hen, for *Carry On*... whichever one it was;
pitched *Orca* to perfection; Peter O'Toole's parrot

and a stag at bay in *Ivanhoe*, lamenting
wasted blood. He hissed in *Alien* at Ripley,
while those old enough still talk of how they hid
behind the sofa from his lion's roar
for Campbell's tinned meatballs, but join

their children, carried off by songbirds Kate Bush
dropped into her enigmatic airs. All him.
More basic was a goat bleat, *On the Buses*,
no match for his wolf which, at the Windmill's
non-stop nude revue, gave everyone the willies.

I recall his coos, plump as a dove's,
on David Nixon's Magic Box; and mum's LP,
played as she helped me shepherd plastic sheep
across the rug – my dad, a stockman's son, unhappy
we'd become so distant from the land.

Raising Steam

i.m. Reginald Gardiner 1903-1980

RADA took toffs, polished them dull, their stock
reduced to *Second Huntsman*, *Lover Spurned*,
The Butler or some Restoration fop.
But airs and graces fed a fire that burned
inside our chap to take *genteel* and make
it locomotive, powered by his knack
for sounding like The Orient Express,
raising the age of steam with every breath:

his clipped delivery of train on track;
the thunder of a tunnel in his chest;
whistles the theatre walls rebounded back;
the pant of a leviathan at rest…

Uncoupled from the poverty of posh,
Reg travelled to Variety, first class.

And They're Off!

i.m. Willy Netta's Singing Jockeys c. *1912*

Sir Laverock in *Le Morte d'Arthur* asked,
What is a man but when he's on horseback?

But what of those who tried and failed to ride
a winner? Stable lads who never made

it past first post, put out to grass, their short
careers reined in. Enter Willy, ticket tout,

barred from the Sport of Kings. Due for some luck,
and musical, our try-again tycoon took

three non-starters – tenor, bass, baritone –
provided silks, caps, britches, billed them

as *Barber Shop Meets Becher's Brook!* They
sang close harmony, while toffs would pay

to piggyback them up and down the theatre
aisles. Bets were placed. Willy's wife sold water.

Night Class

i.m. Dick Emery 1915-1983

I wish I'd seen you sing as Vera Thin,
the forces' sweetheart with a squeak, preferred
by Churchill to the flawless real thing,

and therapeutic after being paired
for far too long with Charlie Drake, who left
you with the shakes, eventually cured

constructing Airfix kits. Restored, you blessed
us with a buck-toothed vicar, College the tramp,
frustrated Hettie and her quest for sex,

camp Clarence in his floral pants, and thanks
for Bump the bovver boy supremely thick
but, better still, that dressing-room hour spent

with you, dead beat, explaining laughter like
a schoolmaster, to set my mind alight.

The World's Greatest Whistler

i.m. Ronnie Ronalde 1923-2015

Listen, this man sent shivers down
Sinatra's spine. Marilyn Monroe
spoke of a state of grace.
But let's go back

to when a boy in Islington blew
Tales from the Vienna Woods
for food, and borrowed birdsong
to return it spotless.

Then the teenager who made
a shilling every triple trill,
enough to fly Stateside where stadia
turned into temples to The Suited Flute.

Rock 'n' Roll drowned Ronnie out,
but whistles as pristine as his
don't disappear. They slip
between the living and the lost;

pipe up again so someone may think
tinnitus at first,
then shut their eyes, untroubled,
in a meadow never mown.

Morton Fraser's Harmaniacs

Mouth organs must be kept from the inept
whose efforts have a butterfly effect.
For instance, *Michael Row the Boat Ashore*,
murdered, makes desert spread a metre more.
Ditto, *Old McDonald's Farm*: note for note,
a piebald nag in Mexico pegs out.
And some insist when unskilled lips accost
Greensleeves, forest the size of Wales is lost.

For God's sake make it stop! My friend, you can,
with any YouTube clip of Morton's men:
ten wizards of the silver wheeze and one
gymnastic dwarf. Press *play* to halt the harm,
and somersault this crippled planet back
to 1966 and *Crackerjack!*

The Man with the Xylophone Skull

i.m. Professor Cheer 1879-1938

Let's hear it for this prematurely bald
headmaster: struck by the disquieting fact
his crown – hit with a brass door-handle – could
resound, a bell, his temples too, he taught

himself to scale an octave, frontal bone
to back, and at the Christmas show knocked out
a carol, *Ding Dong Merrily*, performed,
he quipped (as teachers do) *on high!* But what

should have stayed a daft percussion act at school –
festive morale – didn't. He went on tour,
six years – concussion, mild first, getting worse, till
memory went with his pension, somewhere

old wolves paw at stone, ravens croak, snow falls
on carcasses through which a cold wind howls.

The Ray Conniff Singers

That style Cleo Laine employed
without relent – let's call it song
alarmed. Now picture twenty-five

in orange polyester, turning
Perry Como's *And I Love You So*
into close-harmony hysterics.

Add a family at the cabaret: son affronted
that this hyper-choir were not in hot-pants
(even Nana Mouskouri had a pair);

daughter, older, shoulders shaking;
mum smiling on the ensemble
like she'd been trained in group placation;

dad nodding along and loathing it,
spirit settled in his Parker Knoll back home
and semi-conscious with *The Likely Lads.*

*

We'd no idea this was music at its peak,
more advanced than Mantovani
or a marching band. The only sound,

when not resisted, that could send you
to a state of elevated apathy,
like how religions describe death.

I found out the night that followed,
on my paper round, by trying *Paranoid*,
Black Sabbath, the *bip-di-dee-whap* way.

Phenomenal: the shoulder-strap,
the deeper pain of Sharon Duffy's legs,
that half-out-of-a-hundred in the maths exam,

all syncopated into hiccups on the way
to a far better place, a world
where ordinary words won't do, *be-do!*

Tiddly Om Pom Pom

i.m. Mark Sheridan 1865-1918

Hit after hit, he couldn't kill his gift
for gaiety, the flip, untroubled stuff
men whistled on their way to war – tunes tough
enough for trenches, tears. They made him rich
and wretched, those shape-shifters in his head,
imagined like Beethoven's 5th, dashed out
another *Stop Yer Ticklin', Jock!* instead,
and more top sales to get morose about.

Some say the mediocre can't be spoiled
by anti-climax, but our songsmith died
a death to still all choruses: appalled
beyond condolence by *Beside the Seaside*,
he declared *This last confection breaks my heart*,
and blew his brains out in a Glasgow park.

Slave Song

for Leslie Hutchinson 1900-1969

Black. Baritone. *Breathtaking*, Coward said.
Now let's diminish you with this instead:
Lady Mountbatten so adored your dick,
she got a jewel-encrusted cast of it
from Cartier, to comfort her when you
were entertaining Noel, Novello.

Prohibited from singing on a stage,
you did Cole Porter from the pit, to rave
reviews; received sweets from the royal box.
Received Cole Porter too. But when the facts
about how in demand you were came out,
Lord Louis sued the press and swore in court

No nigger fucks my wife. Cut down, voice gone,
you died selling yourself in Paddington.

Straight Man

You think you could be me, don't you?
The nobody who's only there to prop
the patter up. The one who, deadpan,
asks the obvious to set the silly answers free.

You think you could be me but better.
Make more of an effort. Be a super-feed.
Do so much more than look disdainful.

Try it, then. Try not to smile.
Be subliminal lit by a bank of lights.
Try keeping control, reining in an idiot;
forcing the pace so he can fly.

Try to pitch a put-down perfectly
and, backstage, be the chipper one who copes
with nerves, neurosis. Do the admin too.

Try this for size: the difference between us,
you and me, is I *pretend* I'm dull.
And that barrel of laughs who acts
like he should be locked up –
he is. Try being the key.

Frontiersman

i.m. The Walsall Warrior c. *1879*

By nature, Brummies are morose. They need
shock-therapy at night. So Shaka was
a public good who, following Rorke's Drift,
stormed Moor Street Empire, eyes on fire, white-lipped;
froze misery to solid fear. I've read,
at his last show, he blocked the theatre doors.
This took his audience, captured inside,
out of themselves until the troops arrived.

Once, five police fought hard to inch a friend
of mine toward their transit van, and he
could not stop laughing, knocking hats askew.
I too am taunted: there's a dark, untamed
interior I lack the guts to go to
on my own. Shaka and Greg take me.

The Reluctant Sitter

i.m. Robert Rutherford 1893-1987, entertainer
and Harry Rutherford 1903-1985, artist

Come to paint me? Listen, Harry, can we
rearrange – I've got a show... Oh dear, I see
you're disappointed. Take a seat – *not there!* –
too late – here let me help you off the floor.
No, I built it to collapse like that –
you don't know how to fall, there's a technique.
Give me your hand – oh, sorry, I forgot
mine has a very mild electric shock
strapped to it. Not so mild? Maybe you should wait
a bit – you can't hold brushes with a shake
that bad. Anyway, you've cracked your palette now
but chin up, brother, safe inside your studio,
away from me, I reckon you'll look back
on this and laugh. Call it your own slapstick
routine! You'd rather not? Tell you what,
let's pretend this hasn't happened. You go out
and come back in again... You've hurt your leg?
Roll your trousers up. Right, does it ache
more when I press it? Yes? That's good because
it means it could be worse. Ha! I'll use
that in the act! Please, sit in my chair –
I'll stand until you're feeling better.
Have a little drinkie from this rose...
Sorry, most of that went up your nose –
here's my handkerchief, there's fifty feet
of it – and welcome to my cluttered niche,
my den, my dressing-room without a door,
can't-swing-a-cat comedian's corner.
You look the part, sat there, like you're about

to get yourself made up. Take your coat
off, slip my jacket on. Know any jokes?
No? Surely some snappy anecdotes,
my life in oils? Why not recite one
in the mirror?… Snappy, I said – we'll work on
it. All these hats? I've one for every song
I sing. I make sure they're fittingly wrong:
Be My Sweetheart in a balaclava –
it's the mismatch that provokes the laughter.
Try this topper on. Now tilt it. Brilliant!
Hey, here's a great idea, why don't you paint
yourself, as me? I'll go on stage and do
what I do best. See yourself out. Cheerio.

Anthony Howell and His Disenchanted Sow

They do say never wrestle with a pig,
you both get filthy. So, instead, strip
naked on a busy Belfast street,
assume the crouch of a submissive mate
– porcine-cubic, promising – to woo
(before you're led away) a Tamworth who
has *lovely ginger eyelashes.* Anthony
tried this. The beast, unfortunately,
didn't fancy him – she trotted off to sniff
the crotches of the crowd, an act which
made her vulva swell so much the local paper
featured, for the first time, genitalia;
and squeals from councillors, *If this is art*,
blah blah, ensured it was far more than that.

Largesse

i.m. Teddy Brown 1900-1946

You see, back then, we didn't have *obese*
but *bonny* which, at twenty-seven stone
and three feet wide behind the xylophone,
immaculate in white, wearing a face
full as a plum with pleasure, Teddy was.
Talent as banquet – this boy made light work
of Liszt and jigged with it. He'd bash out Bach
to pirouettes; waltz while he hammered Strauss.

It couldn't last, no feast this lavish can –
their generous nature gets the best of them
some place like Wolverhampton Hippodrome
where, mid-spin, Ted the Plentiful pegged out…
To taste a morsel of his joy, repeat
He's such a size, and so light on his feet!

The Art of Hunger

i.m. Giovanni Succi 1853-1905 and Frances Thomas 1935-1978

Forty days without, *The Fasting Man*
appeared at the Alhambra, Bradford, fresh
from filling halls in Florence and Milan:
Europe's Lord of Famine – in the Flesh!

Propped up by doctors, lost inside a suit
stagehands would strip away to show the lack
of him – translucent under lights – he spoke
in whispers all could hear: *I'm not a freak,*
but one exemplar of the human will
to take control and keep it, breath by breath.

His photograph, all fade and gaze, still
holds the absent presence of an aunt of mine,
less lionised, who starved herself to death –
but she was no phenomenon, 'just vain'.

Praise Poem

i.m. Gracie Fields 1898-1979

Rochdale had never loved like this before,
nor will again. Devotion, raw,
the red meat of it. Gracie tried to keep
things real: travelled by bus and ate

badly. No good. They lionised this lass –
grim adoration growing worse
the more she gave till, rigid with worship,
they lost the faculty to clap,

...and every song I sang felt like a hymn,
she said, *such silence between them,*
full of want – I couldn't let it win, move
me to tears. It's awful but you've

got to weld yourself, body and soul,
into a shield. Retain control.
And after, when you're sitting all alone,
you feel wrung out, frightened, shaken.

So if you think you're hard enough to let
a hill town offer up its heart,
come test your strength. But here's the deal: first sign
of weakness and we'll take you down.

Zazel, The Shooting Star!

i.m. Rosa Richter 1862-1922

Her manager, The Great Farini, was
famous for doing handstands blind across
Niagara, dying over ninety in
his bed. Rosa, fourteen years old, had been
an acrobat since five, but soft bones bend
unprofitably when they've entertained
too long, too soon. His human cannonball
offer, to be the first, could slow the fall
from tumbler to the workhouse – worth a shot.
He gave up the day job while Rosa got
top billing every *maiden flight*, until
she broke her back, which left her in a steel
corset, alone. That's showbiz. All the same,
let's have a galaxy in this girl's name.

Without a Net

i.m. Selina Hunt 1827-1863

Seven months gone, and still walking the wire.
But if you're gifted, with six kids to care
for, there's no easy balance to be struck
between a high-stakes job, and trusting luck
will keep the family afloat. Some said
prenatal ballast might perfect her tread.
Most didn't think that deep, just paid to see
someone soon fit to drop fight gravity.

The day the rope snapped at the Aston fête,
she and her foetus fell for thirty feet.
Bad fortune was blamed, but a panel gave
her eldest boy ten guineas for a grave.
The priest beside it set the record straight:
Selina Hunt had carried too much weight.

Dr Zhivago

Ten. I harbour birthday hopes for
Dr Dolittle at the Savoy.
But Uncle Don, solicitor,

head of the household, never been
a boy, doesn't agree. He's seen
my school report and it's high time

I grew up, got serious, *forthwith.*
So, Dr Zhivago. Uncle's wife,
starvation-diet ageing waif,

is feeling very Julie Christie
in her fox fur coat and hat that she,
despite the artificial heat,

keeps on. Then, in the fight to force
a wafer down her, things get worse:
she faints. The interval's now farce

as dad, general factotum, slings her
like a rug over his shoulder
and advances to the foyer,

followed by a brace of usherettes.
Epic stuff. And that's before my shouts
of *Is there a doctor in the house?*

Power Sharing

i.m. Albert Black 1827-1862

The Man Who Turns To Stone is carbon,
dating, now, in Highgate clay, and set
above his bones the granite cross is not
a landmark in this graveyard ocean
of them, but a totem separate
enough from others to keep concrete what
his iron will accomplished, how the front row
felt, invited onto stage to touch his flesh
made monumental by the mason
in his mind. *By Christ, it was as though*
(one punter said) *his body shot this*
seam of cold through mine and I was taken
to the winter Cairngorms, then became them –
because Albert Black made mountains out of men.

The Dancing Quakers

i.m. Mr Dove and Miss Carman c. *1880*

Friends, and nothing more, despite the gossip,
rampant, when you share a dressing room and put
a sign up, DO NOT KNOCK, WE ARE AT WORSHIP.
That's the nicest word I've seen for it!
Dan Leno quipped, prompting Miss Carman
to respond: *For a comedian*
you have the saddest eyes. Bless you, poor Dan.

The Penny Illustrated said, *On stage,*
until the spirit moves them, they don't move,
creating tension. How this could engage
the patrons at the Gaiety, God knows.
Eventually, all they seemed to do
was *hug a lot, and ask a baffled house*
to join them. Mrs Dove filed for divorce.

Inextricable

i.m. J.H. Walter 1854-1895

Bookies were big fans of this contortionist
who couldn't make ends meet, his debt so bad
he sold his skeleton, was told he had
to take a coffin, with the scientist's
address, who'd own him dead, taped to the lid
wherever he was scheduled to perform,
plus notes instructing stagehands to embalm
his knotted body, given up, gone bust,

but free from what had pared him to the bone:
an unrelenting bent for being crushed,
for inextricable defeat, because
there's nothing more replete than total loss –
the rich, compulsive twist of it I'll bet
no doctor can anatomise, correct.

The Audience

i.m. Les Dawson 1931-1993

I'd never met someone who was no taller
standing up than sitting down. So near the floor
and lacking form, your legend could have been
The Man Without a Chassis!

Little wonder it was hard to find you
in the theatre bar, plonked inside
a ladies' circle being treated
to your *Cosmo Smallpiece* repertoire.

Between the smut and shrieks,
I introduced myself. *Bloody hell, you're big!*
Bloody hell, I shot right back, *you're not!*
A dozen powdered faces froze.

Mine's a double scotch, you slurred,
then turned away. And so did I,
thinking *Fuck this*, but reappeared
with a drink you didn't thank me for.

Les, this was not what I'd expected
when your agent liked my sketches and said
Meet him at the Palace, Manchester.
I'd pictured post-performance bubbly

in your dressing room; chuckles as you loved
my lines; slaps on the back and *Genius!*
Here's to a great relationship!
Instead I'd got a twat, half-cut

in public before curtain-up, who took
my bundle like a summons.
Did Mr Ten Per Cent suggest
when I've time to plough through this?

Another scotch, *And put it on the tab, you twerp.*
When I returned, your groupies had all gone
to take their seats. You pinched a cigarette
and slumped into a grumble

about how Bob Monkhouse hated you
landing 'Blankety Blank':
He coveted that show – still does,
the sun-tanned sack of shite.

Then softer: *Sorry son, I'm not myself.*
The missus… but your punchline was,
she's not got long – and nothing mattered
but to hold her hand.

Trouble is, I love that girl. Still, where there's life…
We almost hugged, then you had to push off
to do your stuff. I hoped you could use mine.
Nothing's impossible, you said, from far away.

Exotica

i.m. Alejandra Dominguez 1791-1833

Madame Zanza, Boneless in the Buff was
also billed, for more upmarket venues,
as *The Filleted Female Nude*. This posh

name was reflected in the ticket price –
her act, of course, the same: total collapse
to form a pile of Puerto Rican flesh,

artiste-as-body-spill, barely above
the footlights, and her dark eyes, crablike, snug
inside the lowest naked fold, would look

this way, then that, at hundreds wondering where
her treasures were concealed among the bare
serpentine softness, foreign, bronzed. We'd stare

hard; she held her shape for seconds, brief enough
to keep us rapt: the span of public love.

Widow Twankey

Daybreak kills the lights along the pier.
Mist at the deep end lifts
and there the Playhouse hangs – that wreck
where last night was the deadest yet: a dozen
plus a seagull on the follow-spot
that took a dislike to his wig,
drawing blood for a finale.

A rock supports a bottle drained of single malt,
and there's a sea breeze dropping salt into his scab.
He's disgraced himself, a cock-stride
from the toilets on the prom –
would have tried to find a gag in that,
the laughter there, back when
he had a name enough to care.

Sea weeps into the dame-shaped crater
made when he lost consciousness,
sometime after they'd paid him off
and said they'll not be wanting him next winter
'cos you're shit, love. Had he thought it might be time
to hang his frock up? B&Q take people on
who haven't got a pension.

Shingle trickles down his knickers.
A crab's been crushed between the scaffolds
of his bra. Around him everything takes shape
as dawn becomes another morning, and it dawns
on him he didn't rip his cheque up on a whim.
Sleek as a private limousine, the tide arrives.
He bows a bit, and starts to wade.

Burlington Bertie

Too late for Vesta Tilly, Ella Shields,
the only women dressed as men I'd seen
would slap their thighs and, à la Gracie Fields,
hit notes like they were purging themselves clean
of song. Dad loved a panto Amazon,
but too much *oomph* could suffocate his son.

Then Christmas 1968 gave me
Anita Harris on *The Good Old Days*,
inside the loosest morning suit she
dared to nearly wear. Low-voiced and with a gaze
so laden and direct my stomach hurt,
through Bertie she breathed *I haven't a shirt.*

This had me taking in more oxygen
than I'd ever required, or will again.

Out from Under

i.m. Kate Cheval 1832-1847

They couldn't crush this girl who knew her place
was at the bottom of a heap of men,
the biggest from the best seats in the house,
hand-picked to form a formal queue of ten,
twenty M'luds, Esquires and Guv'nors not
above making a stately pile on top
of Kate (stepladders helped), a noble effort
by this body of substantial weight
to take her breath away. They'd orchestrate
themselves, a criss-cross hierarchy, and after
their undignified collapse, which found her
flattened but alive, they slapped each other
on the back – *Bad luck, old boy!* – ignoring Kate
of course, who rises now, before us, here.

Mary Poppins

Mum took me. She held my hand throughout
this treat, the night before a darker spell
in hospital to cut a testicle
away, gone rogue and ripe to spread its venom,
take me down. *Hitler only had the one –*
dad's fond response – *don't fuss, you'll be all right.*

But as the lights dimmed in the Odeon
to usher flying nannies, broken kites,
tea parties on the ceiling, Dick Van Dyke's
disguises, fear of the finale grew
inside me, frame by frame: because I knew
the end would come, it's all I focused on,

kept asking *Is it nearly over yet?*
not fooled by soft assurances: *No, sweetheart,*
lots to go. It worked, though, this unhealthy state
of bad enchantment: when Miss Poppins left,
job done, to land on new children bereft
of hope, my loins were so well-girded that

I felt no loss. Unpleasant prospects, when
surrendered to, stop cutting you. I learnt
this as the film wasted itself, and can't
unlearn it; went from cinema to theatre
under no illusions, prepped, already there,
made less: a boy fast-forwarded; a man.

Self Help

i.m. Joseph Grimaldi 1778-1837

Mask off and melancholic, Joseph saw
a doctor who at once prescribed *Grimaldi,*
Mother Goose, Drury Lane – I guarantee
he'll cheer you up! Shuffling to the door,
Joe turned and sighed, *the trouble is, that's me.*
So this joy-bringer of the Regency,
who tickled even Byron, was told to cure
himself by visiting himself. I see

the sense in this corrective double-take:
not navel-gazing like bad poets do,
but an inner trip to introduce you
to the clown behind your frown. Too late
for Joe though: funniest man alive, who died
the only stranger to his sunny side.

Saddled

i.m. Harris 'Wonder Horse' Fitzpatrick 1803-1847

Born to play the front end, under hessian
and felt, Harris expressed such human-equine
feelings, every toss, nod, shake, incline

said more than Hamlet at his most verbose
because, once Harris was immersed in horse,
the stammer didn't matter, for his voice

was body-language – nuzzle, jerk and butt –
a dumb-show of stubborn, affectionate,
skittish, morose. But when he'd got the bit

between his teeth, what started as a hobby
took the reins till, out of season, he
would shy away from words, and nobody

could coax him back: always a danger when
someone feels ill at ease in their own skin.

Better Out Than In

i.m. George Formby Snr 1875-1921

Not the sunbeam with a banjulele
but his dad. Born to a violated child,
he spent more nights than most in sacking
on the doorstep, when they had one.
She'd be inside, out of it. A man,
sometimes about, turned his attention
to whoever was at hand.

Ten when a foundry took him on;
thirteen, tubercular in pubs,
The Wigan Linnet and his chest
played as a double-act that rattled
between *chin-up* ditties.
Coughing champion tonight! he'd chirp,
lost in a costume Chaplin snatched.

At forty-six, backstage, Newcastle Grand,
the people's invalid made light
of bringing *something black up with a spine!*
Then what was left of him collapsed,
leaving a diary full of life,
a book of hits unheard, a healthy boy
to make them *better out than in.*

Beyond Belief

i.m. Sid Field 1904-1950

He talked a good trapeze act – in his tights,
hands white with chalk – the best we never saw:
I might even change my mind, mid-air!
Sid had us gazing at those dizzy heights,
and he was there, all swing and sweep, above us,
never mind he hadn't even climbed
the pole, set foot inside a circus
or off terra-firma, ever. Were we blind

to this pretence? Naïve to let such
elevated promises toss reason
to the wind? Or could Sid's flights of fancy catch
and turn the truth? Can words, well-placed, become
so strong they're flesh and sinew on the wing:
not less than, but beyond the real thing?

Crowd Control

i.m. The Bryn Pugh Sponge Dancers c. *1855*

A soft act to follow? Nothing did –
they always went on last, the *buffer spot*,
when people put their coats on, filtered out
with half an eye on them: *Our job*, Bryn said,
was to prevent a crush, a bottleneck
of bodies heading home. We weren't much good,
see? Some saw that straight away and caught
the early tram. Still, I suppose a few would

hang on till the end, hoping for more than
mattresses three women sank into, sprang from.
There *is* more, though: Bryn married all of them,
you could say on a triple-rebound, then
wrote a memoir, *Ups and Downs*, confessing two
had been his daughters, and the other knew.

Engagement

for George Formby 1904-1961

Last artiste to leave Dunkirk, first back
after D-Day, buck-teeth bared
against the bullets, flat feet tapping

at the double, donkey bray war-cry
above the banjulele's tin-hat rattle…
You got rattled too, outside Berlin,

the celebration show no soldier heard,
drowned out by themselves. Not whistles,
cheers, not well-behaved, but bellows,

frightful, in your face. *Calm down, lads!*
Then the penny dropped: all silly grin
and trivia, you were their instrument –

they roared their want at you, through you,
yelling themselves back from blood
and guts to leaning on a lamp post, home.

Controlled Explosion

i.m. Edgar Kennedy 1890-1948

We called him *The King of the Double-Take*:
glance at – dismiss – think *WHAT?* – stop short – stare back.
Done wrong, the result is a crick in the neck

and no laughs. Your eyes should expand in surprise,
then glisten with rage breaking veins in a face
full of blood pressure: Edgar could raise

his at will so he sweated bright red,
livid beacon. You'll need a bald head
for the next gesture, known in the trade

as a *Slow Burn*, like this: let your hand slap
your crown, spread your fingers, allow them to slip
so they mask then uncover a look fit

to bust – dumb frustration – at what's going on…
Or skip all the above and wallop someone.

Le Pétomane

i.m. Joseph Pujol 1857-1945

From fifteen paces, fart a candle out.
It isn't funny and it isn't clever
though Joseph, his anus trained to hoover air
then blast it free, would disagree: his heart
set on conveying it's an ill wind
that blows no French trouper any good – and art,
I'd argue, should be felt first in the gut.
Anyway, he made a bomb, then opened
his own bakery, the sign saying – in French –
An empty vessel never makes most noise!
Henry the Second's fool, another
flatulist, and French again, fared rather
better with a dukedom and one-tenth
of Kent, still passed on through the eldest boys.

Castrato

i.m. Carlo Farinelli 1708-1782

Had I not been cut,
I would have grown up half the man
that I became – a peasant
with dependants on the breadline,
and a wife no longer touched
by overtures. Myself unable
to interpret hers.

Talented, they took me young,
prised me apart, promised
the loss would put meat
on my parents' table. On our bones.
This proved accurate: the business
of an instant with a burning blade
kept winters warm.

Dosed with opium, the days I bled
were my only silent ones.
But how can I sing to you, so far away
and deaf to me, of lifelong adoration –
operatic; dresses to die for
and a sound so beautiful,
I'd leave you weeping for your inner child.

Tragedian

i.m. Richard Burbage 1568-1619

Hit me again! I love it. Let me rise,
then beat me back. Make it my fault: a plague
of tortured Moors, Macbeths, Hamlets and Lears
on me! The drop, from deity to knave,
so steep my stomach, crown get left behind;
that rocket ride designed to crash; the hope,
fear, hate on board, the sorrow: I was born
for this. Bipolar fortune on a loop.
So dig me up, cast me in plays about
the brief but great your killjoys denigrate
and bury. Hancocks. Larkins. Bests. Relight
my fire to fight and lose for them: I'll take
success and turn it sour, to entertain
the lucky dull, the smug. Hit me again!

Nightmare Scenario

i.m. Richard Dadd 1817-1886

In Dickens' day the disenchanted fled
to Fairyland. Hungry for it, they paid
bread-money entrance into Drury Lane,
where Dadd's vast panto backdrops fast became
more popular than Cinders, Puss or Dick
who hated the ovations his dark
images of elven glades received –
no entertainer likes to be upstaged
by scenery: it made them mad, but nowhere
near as mad as Dadd, obsessed by the idea
his palette set free poltergeist who had,
in turn, possessed his father, so he stabbed
him dead. In Broadmoor, allowed only oils,
he painted pixies, weeping, on the walls.

Lo! Hear the Gentle Lark

She cleared the Underground with that,
or would have if the Air Raid Wardens
hadn't barred the exits.

So many wartime party pieces,
freed from parlours, wrapped the Circle Line
in misery, and hers was one

of London's worst, survivors said.
Which makes me ask, when victory denied
her train wreck of a turn its platform,

did she travel north, distorting choirs,
then bump into my mum, tone-deaf in Manchester
but desperate to audition for *No, No, Nanette*?

Was this the woman who called twice a week
to prove two voices could be twice as bad as one;
why dad signed up to join The Stoic's Arms

darts, billiards and bowls leagues, leaving me
perched on a pouf and grinning, fingers in my ears,
learning early to enjoy an awful time?

Foreign Exchange

i.m. Guillaume Stout 1778-1821

This *Gallic boulevardier*, whose voice
was neither flat nor strangled, more a cross
between them, wasn't Guillaume at all,
but Bill, sometime dog-oil supplier, Goole.
Upfront, at least, he let his public know:
My popularity is now so low,
I'm going to Frenchify my name, because
they're hated less than me. How wrong he was,

but what a coup: ladies who lunched began
to put him on display in their *At Home*
events, where patriotic men could shout
abuse, flash steel his way. A racing hit,

he raised his tariff, was richly despised
and hacked to bits the day Bonaparte died.

Counter Culture

i.m. Charles Olden 1905-1977

As *Wigan's Own Musician-Raconteur*
Charles Olden, ten years in, had got nowhere:

even the Krusty Krab cancelled on him.
So he reversed his surname and became

Nedlo, Gypsy Fiddler! and the rest
is history. Out went the formal dress –

winged collar, dicky, cummerbund – in came
a red bandana, buckles; Beethoven

was ditched for jigs, flat anecdote for cheek,
which got him lots of sex as well, despite

his weight. Try it – identify what's wrong
and turn it back to front. Treat all you've known,

held sacrosanct, with utter disrespect
and we may take you seriously yet.

Brass Band

Bottom line? Seconds into *Sailing*
I'm in tears. Two bars, as a rule, before
the waters break and all my sorrows
drown, diffuse into church hall,
assembly room. It works as well for any tune
dipped in your mournful warmth.

I'm trying to say I love you, and I don't care
if you hit me with *The Stripper* or *Hey Jude* –
who else takes air to make compassion
hospitals have targets for? Then there's your faces,
blank and only blowing; outfits so all the same,
braided or plain, they break my heart.

I've seen you seated, standing, on the march;
in junior schools fresh and lamentable;
as engineers all male and overweight; Welsh Asians
adding spice to *Bread of Heaven* – and always
I'm delivered back, a boy of four, found on the prom
in Bridlington, not lost, just listening.

Pleasure Craft

i.m. Russ Conway 1925-2000

From choirboy to borstal, where he taught
himself to hammer a piano and got
Bobby Shafto off so well, the governor
transferred him, sixteen, to a minesweeper.

Four years close-quartered told him he was gay,
hooked him on eighty cigarettes a day
then tossed him back to shore, a wreck, but with
a repertoire, *Fun Songs for in the Bath.*

Fame followed, so did a recurrent dream
of drowning: dead inside, he tinkled on
– think Mrs Mills meets Edgar Allan Poe –
and when Sasha Distel complained *That guy*
just grabbed me by the throat! I hope it's true
the answer came *Worse things happen at sea.*

Response

Joe Loss, dapper as a cat, pivots from
his band to face a crowd as uniform,
together, but less polished, more fatigued.
Servicemen, he beams, *now I'm going to lead*
you in a singalong. Then he tells them
all to clear their throats, *like this, a-hem!*
Proof positive of patronising twat
comes with *Can everybody manage that?*

Yes Sir! This flank of damaged lads, who took
their doctorates in coughing at Dunkirk,
launch all they've left into a repertoire
of phlegm-evacuation. Half an hour
of bronchial *a cappella*, mucus morse
code. Rough interpretation: *Kiss my arse.*

Bad Rap

i.m. Leonard Norris 1935-1978

Len, lathe operator, played
the flugel horn, but factory brass bands
could mask an undertone, darker,
felt in his bones after the union
marched to a closed-shop tune
and he chose to be deaf to it,
refusenik, so received the silent
treatment, years of it, spat at,
then someone left a manhole open,
someone shoved him from behind.

Why should I care?
Len was my uncle and I watched
him never work or play again,
unable even to eat peas,
mashed up – nobody faced
the music – so don't rhapsodise
about working men's clubs to me:
some stripped the brave
of their ability.

Roughage

i.m. Bombastus Furioso c. *1820*

To entertain us during scene changes,
Bombastus ate a chest of drawers each night
throughout a run of *Where's My Helmet?* famous
for its fifteen acts. *This is a sight*,
a critic said, *to more than compensate*
for wooden acting and a rotten plot.
I'm told cabinet makers would compete
amongst themselves to build one that could not
be splintered into dinner by his teeth.
He finished off the lot, followed by a plaque,
Our furniture has Furioso beat!
In later life, he fell apart – like
flatpacks do today – and died in a secure
unit chewing both his arms red raw.

Three Sightings of Batman

I *Stretford Co-op 1968*

Surprisingly short; waist-high
to the manager who marched him out,
red in the face and cape askew.

A pity, when the day began so well,
with word the Farley's Rusks were going
walkabout again. A minor crime
to some, not him. So he patrolled
the aisle, his kit a size too big,
but every circuit saw him growing into it.

When stopped at last and asked what
he was playing at, *Being Batman*
didn't seem to satisfy. Flustered,
he added *I'm protecting baby food.*

Hauled to a small dark room, he found,
inside his costume, he had lost
his tongue – but kept a grip on tears
until he was unmasked.

II *Kendal Milnes Department Store, Manchester* 1992

HAVE YOUR PHOTOGRAPH TAKEN WITH BATMAN!
Late December? Had he captured Santa,
occupied his grotto, stripped
it back to cave? And why no smile,
when all who posed wore grins?
Grown men in the main.
He'd shot up, though – the suit
a better fit, but pinched a bit
around the middle or *bat gut.*
Short term, perhaps, but sentry-still
he stood, legs parted, next to Lingerie.
Handy for tights, someone observed.
He didn't like that, you could tell.

III *Stockport Town Hall Roof* 2003

Another sign, this time
FATHERS FOR JUSTICE. Like him,
it looked unsafe. Below,
a less arresting uniform
called up *Come down, you berk!*

Back in bother, then? Not the best
role model for the kids.
Icons should offer something
positive. Or was that what he was
aiming at, before he slipped?

The Hard Stuff

i.m. Joseph Frank 'Buster' Keaton 1895-1966

Not played with, till his parents tipped him up,
arse over tit, at six: *The Human Mop!*
Jesus! This kid could save the act! A gift
for keeping rigid as his head was dipped
into the bucket wrung possessive pride
– a new-born soppiness for what they'd made –
from two who, in the dock as child-abusers,
stripped their asset to reveal no bruises

and the rest we know: once on his feet,
Buster tumbled to success, got wet
a lot, which may be why his greatest trick,
he said, was *crawling from a bottle, more dead*
than alive... I sweated myself dry, instead
of drowning, an old soak, *like father had.*

Little Wonder

i.m. John Maskelyne 1839-1917

Your magic baffled us, but then you said
and now I'm going to show you how it's done.
No, John! Not one of your believers cared
how you could levitate Tutankhamun,
or where the lady vanished. All you did
was turn a dumbstruck audience into
an angry mob. We wanted to be had,
hoodwinked, not disenchanted. And did you

have to smash our faith in séances as well?
Soulless, your exposures. So good riddance
when you got a new career to build
the first coin-in-the-slot public convenience,
which prompted Madame Lilly, medium,
to say *let's lock the tosser up in one.*

Go Gentle

i.m. Gilbert Harding 1907-1960

Pompous, irascible, he found fame
as the Rudest Man in Britain,
exploding every week on *What's My Line?*

Few knew this unforgiving Cambridge man
came from an unforgiving children's home,
sent there – dad dead – his mum's unwanted son.

But sympathy would have been fatal when
ten million of us were tuning in
each episode, in love with hating him.

The pay was great, the cost was too, as he became
our favourite public enemy, relied upon
to keep a bad show breaking records, number one,

until he died outside Broadcasting House, soon
after he'd confessed on air, *I'm so alone.*

Street Cred

i.m. Tony Warren 1936-2016

Pendlebury bred its women wartime
tough. Mams, aunties, grans, *the flamin' neighbours* –
warriors with nowt who would not ration
what they were: gossip, stoic, glamour puss;

grafter, scrubber, put-upon. They brought you
up, my lad – Eccles Grammar clever,
lippy, witty, out-and-proud before
it was allowed: love on the never-never.

Future? Fallow at first. *Children's Hour*, a script
for Biggles and, expelled from acting class,
a spot of choreography in strip
clubs – hardly Moulin Rouge, but ready cash.

Later, sleeping on a slow train home from
Thanks, but no in London, you awoke – and how!
I'll write about Florizel Street! Hang on,
a tea lady (relation, maybe?) saw

the flaw: *Sounds like a disinfectant, son.*
So, *Coronation.* Chicken? Could you get that
back in '59? Not down your way, young man,
barely turned twenty-one, about to take

those matriarchs and make them Elsie, Ena,
Annie… Ken? Wrong gender, kid, but maybe
he was you: bright boy; back-alley dreamer.
Light of Manchester. Making history.

The Man Who Killed Houdini

i.m. J. Gordon Whitehead 1895-1954

I was thirty. Still a student. Immature.
The only chains I'd wrestled with were
theoretical. And what a lark to lie
my way into his dressing room. To see
him semi-naked, dabbing pancake
on his face. Average, unshackled – no great
shakes. Like me. But foolish – happy to be
hit: *Hard as you can, boy*. Boy? *Just give me
time to brace myself.* Like hell! Four
punches to the stomach, he was on the floor,
doubled-up and writhing. Not an act.
Ruptured appendix – boy – get out of that!
His tomb's impressive, but my pauper's grave
attracts the masses. People are depraved.

Here's Looking At You

i.m. Alice Wolfenden 1861-1913

Chaplin called movement *liberated thought.*
No words required. *Action is all.* But what
if you distil a lifetime's liveliness –
the ducks and dives, embraces, feints; compress
every advance, retreat, escape, into
one concentrated stare, directed through
the theatre's gloom; let your eyes only tell
a tale of non-stop doings – heaven, hell?

Alice mastered this. Completely still, she'd throw
her gaze across the footlights. Those who
held it were transported – felt again
all that had lifted, stirred or broken them.
Hers was the first act women came in groups
to watch, and sob. We men studied our boots.

Lament

i.m. Sing Something Simple 1959-2001

Sunday afternoons gave up the ghost
to this: a lone accordion
held little comfort as the theme tune
faded into half an hour of shadow,
cast across the country
by the Light Programme.

It came to rival *Songs of Praise*
for sudden deaths:
the tender preface could have been
Why not lie back
and ponder ways to end
it all without alarming others.

At eight I joined a boxing club
that met when it was on the radiogram.
An expert might conjecture
I preferred a fat lip to Cliff Adams
and his choir, for over forty years
kept artificially alive:

that's ten prime ministers,
all looking grim. The folk who tuned in
first, from choice, are falling now.
But they were tough – took any measure
of *make-do* thrown at them,
could survive on airwaves if required.

Buccaneer

Jack Drake, blacksmith by day, tenor at night,
went through the *Pirates of Penzance* cast like
a coach-and-four. Man, woman, stagehand, star,
it mattered not what character you were –
he had the whole ensemble in his sights;
performed, hammer-and-tongue, for thirty nights.

Backstage, the atmosphere was fraught with tears,
recriminations, jealousies, and fears
of STDs – quite a baptism for
myself, debuting as the cabin boy.

It's rare, in G&S, to come across
a player with the least appeal. What was
it Jack possessed that captured all of us?
Perhaps he practised on his customers.

Double Act

Amanda! Keith! Our hug spanned eighteen years
since that night at *The Rocky Horror Show*
with Nicholas Parsons, queen of comperes
in suspenders, your borrowed PVC so
tight it split, and me hidebound by leather
trousers shrunk the size of lederhosen
in the wash. Was love suppressed by laughter?
Take the incident in that Italian,
after *La Cage aux Folles*, our second date,
when you mistook a store room for the loo
but couldn't find the light until you'd wet
yourself and, when you told me, I did too.
Only a pair of theatre trips, then we
were parted. Just for fun, let's make it three.

Scandal

i.m. Frank Randle 1901-1957

Cirrhosis couldn't kill him on its own:
Death had to call a combo in – pneumonia,
TB, acute gastritis and the clap –
to see this fucker off who cut his comic teeth

at twenty-one by ripping out the lot
with pliers and a bucketful of scotch,
then filled his boots with pebbles for a year
till I was crippled like a proper clot,

and twice a day he'd bowl his body down
the cellar steps, *to get it right*, found infamy,
a flagrant wife, paid private dicks who stalked
and shagged her while her *mad-head man*

wrecked auditoria but kept his dressing room
pristine, and impresarios sent cash
so he would not appear impromptu, but he did,
and once, before the bench, he turned a judge

into a thumb-sucker, got off, and made his troupe
extract their gnashers too – *get some integrity!* –
then sacked them all because they couldn't sink
a crate of ale each and perform, so if you're sick

of entertainers wanting hugs, applause,
for being *in recovery*, their faces like wet bread,
boohoo, no guts to spill but still they do, meet Frank
who bit the dust so *bloody blessed*, and weep.

Vintage

i.m. Jimmy James 1892-1965

Teetotal, but *I'll play the best drunk yet!*
he pledged, waving a crumpled cigarette,
gone out, as counter-balance to collapse;
red face a map of utterly relaxed
bewilderment – every sated muscle slack
except the eyebrows; promise and loss caught
in his bent carnation. Jimmy scored a hit

and you can too: fake it to make it;
act as though you're wasted, an inebriate
who doesn't give a shit who knows; ensure
your rivals watch you walk into a door
but, on the other side, be stone-cold sober,
sorted, focused. Stagger and confound them:
land the job, don't lose the kids, the car, the home.

Clever Bugger

i.m. Bob Monkhouse 1928-2003

Why did we laugh, but never love you, Bob?
Some claimed you came across as insincere.
So what? You were a comic, not the pope.
Perhaps that calculated gulp before
each punchline, patter too precision-made,
anecdotes too pleased with one another,
plus your business acumen and tan, said
Clever Bugger never *National Treasure*

till, with weeks to live, bloated and slow from
drugs, you begged all men, on *Parkinson*,
to take a prostate test. Too late for you,
but what a warm performance, funny too –
it won us critics over there and then:
smart move, Bob, dying *such a decent man*.

Civic Theatre

Essential to the town's supply of ham
and never known to not deliver, here
Macbeth, La Cage aux Folles, See How They Run

have all been butchered, served up overdone
to friends and relatives, the latest mayor
essential to the town's supply of ham.

How seamlessly the shows flow into one
homogenous creation – *Who Goes Bare,*
Macbeth, La Cage aux Folles, See How They Run,

but each with unexpected extras in:
startled stagehands, Banquo falling through his chair,
essential to the town's supply of ham.

And every set unfailingly Am Dram –
potted plants, French windows, even in *Hair,*
Macbeth, La Cage aux Folles, See How They Run.

Soon it's *The Crucible*. That should be fun.
I'm in the chorus, do support us, we're
essential to the town's supply of ham!
Macbeth! La Cage aux Folles! See How They Run!

Hostess Trolley

Often employed in Alan Ayckbourn plays,
this one, as soon as it was wheeled on stage,
loaded with nibbles, drinkie-poos, began
to concertina. Which it would, when some
fool hadn't locked the catch. Geoffrey, who no
amount of pancake could remould into
a suave young architect, couldn't let go
of it throughout the second act. Where he
went, it went, and the bending made his tight
suit trousers look half-mast. Then his back seized.
During the interval, we tried some holds
and tugs that made it worse. He's still not right,
we've heard: no one from our lot ever sees
him, now he's cast so well for playing bowls.

Dumbing Up

Here's a tip: don't cast an academic
as a panto character. In *Sinbad* we
made this professor the Sultan a'Cake:
a full rehearsal wasted by the fuss
he made about the most historically
correct way his harem should serve him grapes.
Can we consult? More hours lost because
his costume seemed *I'm sorry, far too late*
for the Abbasad Caliphate. First night,
distracted by a book, thick as a brick,
by Freud, *Unconscious Humour*, he forgot
to put his contact lenses in which meant
he wrecked the set. Chaos. Light entertainment,
sad to say, makes fools of men who think a lot.

Town Crier

Hang on, I know him: under that three-cornered hat
and fulsome cloak stood Frank – old classmate,
animal – who, massive at fifteen,

found me half-naked in the changing room,
scooped me up and, singing *Diamonds Are Forever*,
tossed me like a towel into the showers.

This because I'd joined a cycling club,
which Frank decided made me homosexual.
The Head suggested *Francis can be boisterous.*

Boisterous. Listen, most violence never bothers me:
a blow, if well-received, can border on enjoyable.
But when Frank struck, you wouldn't be on solids

for a fortnight. After school, he went inside –
assault – then to the builder's merchants
where he'd overfill and hurl two sacks of aggregate

at once onto my truck, his look divulging
how he longed to add me to the tally.
Now, approaching pension age and run to fat,

he's in the Civic Centre, wringing the neck
of a bell, licensed at last to cause alarm,
make children cling to mums who stoop and flinch.

Light Brigade

i.m. Macauley's Leaping Infants 1856-1866

Alive, but both legs left at Balaclava,
lance corporal Macauley swore he'd rather
starve than beg: perhaps pride came before

and following a fall, for men who'd been
with the Six Hundred and survived. His plan
was martial: muster local urchins lame

from twisted, short or withered limb, club foot,
rickets – plus those born whole who later got
what they deserved – then teach them theirs was not

to reason why, when he said *Jump*, but ask
How high? The *Times* claimed it could never last,
yet England's Most Unlikely Acrobats

toured ten years without praise: laughter, instead,
kept both Macauley and his army fed.

Speech Coach

i.m. George Gorin 1853-1884, and his Pedalling Princesses

Thrown by his bike (they can sense dislike), how
did George, born lacking balance, train ten girls
all saddled with an orphan's weight of no
means left, no way ahead, to ride two wheels
en masse? How was he able to impart,
with words alone, the wherewithal to form
a tower of themselves, a work of art
in leotards, too sure to topple; turn
them on the farthing of his faith, their need;
from fallen, talk them flawless, in three years,
to fame? And can this man be classified
as a Svengali of the handlebars?
Practitioner of cog-psychology?
What manner of trick cyclist was he?

A Funny Thing Happened…

i.m. Frankie Howerd 1917-1992

Every quip fresh from the quipperies!
Fresh? All right, let's just say *pre-loved.*
But you try being new, looking like me –
the man who lied about his age, *adding* years
to match the lines. Try sweating for six decades –
comeback after comeback since your first
No! Missus! Nay! Thrice nay! Titter ye not!

Before the flops, I thought who wouldn't flock
to watch a gossip in a toupée waffle?
What's not to like? *Face like a bankrupt nag*,
a critic said. My mother, actually.
Bless her, we shared so much. But even she
had no idea her son was gay: in those days
it was bitter out. I hid it well. No?

I must confess backstage perhaps I fell
a little short of coy. Clinically depressed,
it seemed to help. What didn't was a shrink
from Harley Street who fed me LSD
before a romp around his attic every weekend.
Best cure for your stage fright,
he'd cackle, catching his breath.

Triumphs? *Frankie Howerd Meets The Bee Gees*
wasn't one. Thank God for the Oxbridge set
who dug me up again. *Alternative*, they called me –
how we laughed. A judge dug up my lover too.
Exhumed him from our mock Egyptian tomb.
Now there's a tale that might have packed 'em in.
Too late – my lips are sealed.

Dun Roamin'

i.m. Gerald Butterworth 1857-1919

In boots, long socks with garters, khaki shorts,
he'd bellow songs about the Great Outdoors
and, yes, though tubby and by no means tall,
the strapping voice and big hat made us all
think *Here's a giant of a man*, for whom
those cardboard hills on stage, fake thunder from
the wings, buckets of rainfall, posed no threat:
he laughed at them, we laughed with him, yet

we alone continued laughing after
Baden-Powell invited him to take
some Cub Scouts (*briskly, mind*) up Langdale Pike,
and Gerald's legs gave way, requiring four
small boys, first-aiders, one for each limb,
to ferry him, dead silent, down again.

Confidence Trick

i.m. Felicitous Bob Franklin 1831-1878

All Bob could do was brag. Songs, handsprings, gags,
a basic jig – beyond him. Proper acts,
proud to dress difficult as easy, spat
his name. But in the gods we couldn't get
enough of this enigma, trousers
ragged as those hanging from the worst of us:
Despite my great success, I won't lord it,
he crowed, *over you less fortunate.*

Bollocks, of course. Deep down we must have known
he didn't own a racehorse, let alone
Grange-over-Sands, but his gift was to make
us *wish* he did, and when he said good luck
may never come our way, we'd smile, *he's right*,
until we hit the street, then fights broke out.

Caretaker

He had no name, this bucket-carrier,
curmudgeon, always bending to unblock a drain,
brush up, bleed radiators, and the rumour was

he'd lost his toes, the lot, in World War Two –
that's why his walk had so much rock,
a toddler's forward progress.

Laughable. The type of man we didn't want
to turn into but, knowing our luck, would –
and I'd be lying if I claimed, for me,

this changed when, through a tiny pane
of smash-proof glass, I watched him in the gym
collecting balls and hoops, before he nudged,

as if by chance, the tape recorder on.
To *Morning Song* by Grieg,
he started swaying, slightly, out of sync,

half-off the margin of a mat he hadn't cleared.
His arms began to lift, not much, a bashful flap,
a reticent romancing of the music.

Maybe half a minute passed, with nothing
added to the repertoire until he wiped
his eyes and stood, head bowed.

I'm still not sure what made me walk away
so slowly down the corridor, or how I knew
to broadcast what I'd seen would hurt us both.

Immense

i.m. Little Tich 1867-1928

To stunt the growth, to kill not cure, cast out
a boy with webbed hands who's discovered on
some train line where he's cried so hard his bag
of sweets, bought with a final penny, has
congealed. Make him Victorian – reason
enough to stop at four feet six and doubt

the prospect of old bones. How long would be
the odds on one so lost learning to dance;
in boots the length of him perfect *en pointe*
to such extent, even Nijinsky went
as far as *genius* – and what's the chance
of mastering ten instruments, be three
times married, mistresses… Reverse this, ask
is anything beyond a great man's grasp?

Above All

i.m. Clarence Willard 1882-1962

Billed as *The Man Who Grows*, he rose to fame
stretching himself – mind over skeleton –
then cantilevered back again, his spine
a hybrid: column and accordion
because – born paralysed, left side – Clarence
became a human rack, employed this trick
through childhood as his vaudeville defence
against exclusion, pity, getting hit.

So if, like mine, your stature varies day
by day, depending on how high or low
friends and the bloody rest reset the bar,
be Clarence: make the ebb and flow they see
come from a place beyond their harm; let no
less able oafs control how tall you are.

Vera

Even then it was a name for adults,
not an eight year old. In the backward stream,
worse at maths than me, she had no father

and a limp. Her mum was Mrs Worthington,
so we'd stand at her broken gate and sing
Don't put your daughter on the stage, then run

until, one teatime, more worse for wear
than normal, Mrs W came round to shout
our antics at my dad. He listened –

placidly for him – before responding
Fair enough, but she's hardly Tiny Tim.
I had a stab at fending off the strap with:

Vera doesn't mind, she says she likes it.
Her mum's drunk all the time and starves the dog.
If you don't hit me I'll apologise.

Before they took her into care, Vera performed
a vent act for the teacher with her Sindy doll
to Neil Sedaka's *Where the Music Takes Me*,

ending on a *happy happy happy happy day!*
that left the class light-headed with respect
and must have taken years of practice.

Eleven, Plus

for Freddie Parrot-face Davies

In retrospect, to wear a bowler hat
so low his ears bent double, then displace
each S by blowing raspberries, was not
Oscar material but, in the days
when train-impersonators hadn't yet
been shunted off, nor musclemen in trunks
with organ music, Freddie's speech defect
could fill a seaside theatre's summer months.

I loved that man, unaware my laughter
led my best friend's gifted younger sister,
who read Brontë, to believe I was backward,
until I asked her to go out with me
years afterwards, and she didn't say no,
just looked appalled before responding *You?*

Stepping Out

i.m. Jack Beckitt and His Talking Shoes 1925-2010

Variety was dying on its feet:
in Blackpool bad comedians between
sullen striptease was called a *Summer Show* –
no place for an unfashionably clean
ventriloquist, until Jack Beckitt,
booed off stage, tripped over a stiletto
and she spoke to him. His down-at-heel brogues
thought *gorgeous!* and replied – tongue-tied, polite –
which made her feel complete again. Jack took
the threesome from Cleckheaton to Las Vegas
for their honeymoon, where Caesars Palace
fell for footwear so in love, so hand-in-glove,
who yodelled *That's Amore* – and before
too long the patter of bootees was heard on tour.

The Belly Dancers of Burnage

There wasn't one objection to the Tesco store:
no shops or heritage to save, no nature
nestling between dual carriageways.

Rumours *Oasis* were to grace the opening
– the Gallaghers grew up here, that's why
they sound like that – proved false

and, truth be told, the women were bussed in
from Whalley Range. A bit slack and shambolic
but you had to give them ten for effort.

When a jazz band upped the ante with *Chicago*
some of us, me in the main, began to cry.
Pride, you see – we had a taste of it that day.

Crossing the Floor

Last night I was a Tiller Girl again:
these realignments in my sleep, once rare,
are stepping up, a regular routine
which, as a man of habit, I prefer –
and maybe kicking sixty is the age
half-cock conservatives don't cast aside
the orthodox, but seek to disengage
a bit and hit a less prudential stride.

So tuck me in and turn me loose among
those level heads and feathers; dress my dreams
with deviance I can depend upon –
extravagant yet safe inside the bounds
adhered to by my sisters – and I'll be
no maverick but moderately free.

The Highland Live-Wire

i.m. Walford Bodie 1869-1939

What set his name in lights was when he got
the audience to strap him down and shoot
ten thousand volts, twice-nightly, through him.
Ladies fainted from the stink of singeing skin;
Houdini, *shocked like I've never been before*,
sent the original electric chair
from Sing Sing as a gift. How charming.
Fired up now, Bodie began claiming
he could heal the sick: *Send me your lame,*
your simpletons, I'll fry them whole again!
or words to that effect, and Aberdeen saw
hundreds turn up to be cured. Some were,
but proper doctors branded him a quack –
then practised ECT: pot, kettle, black?

Hostilities

i.m. Lew Stone 1898-1969

Bandleader Lew was called *our little Jew*
by toffs who saw the war out in the *bomb-proof*
Dorchester where concrete, castle-thick,
ensured the jazz played gaily on, despite
Luftwaffe night-attacks, flicked off like specks
of dust from concierges' overcoats.

What larks the fortified progressive set,
safe under girders, braced by glitz, got
up to through our darkest hours to keep
their peckers up: the *arse-and-fanny club* deep
in the private crannies of the reinforced
gymnasium. *No Yids allowed, of course –*

Dame *Chandelier-Earrings* Granville,
flame-haired Hitler fan, made that the only rule.
In other rooms and on the dance floor,
Cecil Beaton saw *expensive squalor –*
even Ernest Hemingway, no less,
trying, at least, to look androgynous.

The press reported that a *rich old Hebrew*
was *bamboozled* by a *clever whore*;
Duff Cooper and Lord Halifax behaved
like rations don't apply to the depraved,
sniggering to silk-pyjama'd mistresses
about Blanche 'Duffy' Dugdale, *Zionist*,

whilst table-talk would often turn to
what we think of incest, which didn't do
a thing for Orde Wingate, whose preference
for bonhomie dished out as violence
once forced him to slap Lew on the back
so hard, Orde wanked about it for a week.

And what of Lew, who had to entertain
these *washed-up Riviera sweepings* when,
outside, they wouldn't be seen dead with him?
Well, his baton waved its thanks each time
they paid for a request in cash Lew sent
to friends fleeing from worse imprisonment.

I'm Here All Week!

So every Sunday platforms crawled
with acrobats and mimics, comics,
rope-dancers and whistlers, human flies
and living skeletons who'd bonded
– band call, matinees and twice a night –
now forced once more to say farewell.

Black-face minstrels, ladder-climbers,
dentalists and paper-tearers, torn asunder
– limb from fellow nifty limb, dab hand,
anarchic twinkle, idiotic grin –
all waiting to be freighted, towns
and troupes apart, to far-flung
Empires, Grands and Hippodromes.

Take stock of them, these seventh-day itinerants,
transports of delight; imagine family
that falls apart as soon as it's been formed,
belonging broken-up each time the trunks
are packed; departure on departure,
till it gets too tough for some, who turn
to face the station wall: *Enough. End of the line.*

Let's label them the Sabbath Gone, those conjurors
who vanished behind banks of steam;
strong men curled small on metal benches;
infant prodigies lost long before they disappeared –
and look in local rivers: you can still find scraps
of costume, cape, snagged on a willow
root, rinsed of all wonder, colour, life.

All the Rage

i.m. Drayton Goodsir 1821-1883

Drayton sang a single line, *Let's Shake On It!*
incessantly. What started soft and low
rose to crescendo, then yell, as he leapt
into the auditorium and pumped
– like it or not – each punter's hand, row
after row. Tough love? Affection-as-affront?
The Stage called it a *domino effect*
of bonhomie. Maybe. But fellowship,
boiled up to pressure-cooker pitch, can blow,
so when, rampant by now, he roared *I want*
you, urge you, to go further and embrace
your neighbour! hugs, backslaps were soon replaced
by shoves, then fists, the free-for-all complete when
St John's Ambulance Brigade weighed in.

Chanteur

i.m. Charles Aznavour 1924-2018

Fed up with feeling optimistic?
Put Charles on, whose height, or lack of it,
was one of the few things he laughed about.

That, and being named, time and again,
The World's Best-Known Armenian.
But what about Tigron Petrosian?

he'd ask, aware the entertainment press
don't follow chess that avidly. *Your loss,*
and mine, his lived-in, long-abandoned face

would gift us, and this was *his* gift: to share
in melancholy tenor, not despair
but something softer, more finessed, more

French – the *c'est la vie* when post-coital bliss
can't sleep us through sterility, divorce
or, worse, lyrics that lovingly rehearse

a prostate diagnosis, drunken
days; even a song in celebration
of the European Union,

wrung through his bruised vibrato, sounded so full
of sorrow for how hard first love can fall,
Edith Piaf lent President de Gaulle

her handkerchief. *I'm paid per sob*, he told
Le Figaro. Perhaps his own could
be traced back to twenty, when he sheltered

Jewish families, their lives and his at risk.
Listen to *She*, hear how bleak happiness
can be: there's more than artistry to this.

Memory Man

i.m. Herbert Fernandez 1813-1898

We all recalled his glory days, before
grey whiskers: *Ask me anything!* Facts filled
Hull Hippodrome, staccato-sharp and sure –
no doubt about the data he revealed;
his mind as rich as any bank – robust
beyond belief. But why, in later life, when
age ate his reserves and he stood at a loss,
did no one treasure Herbert less, or blame
him playing to our faith instead of trust?
Why weren't his nightly clangers billed, at best,
as laughable: what makes ovation last?
Let's call it love, and hope, when we become
befuddled by our audience, uncertain,
our performance isn't mocked, but smiled upon.

Soul Mates

i.m. Arthur Rickett d. 1883

Arthur created characters then he,
quick-change, became them: dirty bugger
Gunter Rummage; missionary Reverend Zeal;
little tyke Bob Scrap; Caruso Blubber,
crackpot, whaler; the unbearable Jack Strutt...
I could go on – he did, and off, and on again
two dozen times in fifteen minutes, but
each concentrated cameo contained

a rich existence so fleshed-out, complete,
on Arthur's deathbed he enquired about
the health of all of them, and some turned up
to say farewell, so I suggest it's not
dead relatives we reach to touch when
our own curtain falls, but everyone we've been.

That's Your Lot

i.m. Tubby Turner 1882-1947

Tubby Turner's trick was to fail to put
a deckchair up then, in a temper, chuck
the bloody thing away. But somehow, through
the flap and rattle of its flight, it did
what Tubby demonstrably couldn't do,
and clattered back on stage unfolded, fit
for sitting in. But Tubby never sat,
despite a disappointed public who
clamoured for the climax of a seat
collapsing underneath a heavyweight.
Instead, he'd amble over and pretend
he was about to park himself, but then
just bow. A big name like him knew, with fare
this poor, you've got to leave 'em wanting more!

NOTES

The Opener (11): *Don's Inebriated Dart-Blowers* once went on a pre-performance rampage, puncturing bicycle tyres in Swansea.

Juvenile (12): Georgie Doonan continued his bottom-kicking act into adulthood, and even starred in films, doing nothing different.

Coming On Strong (13): Although very slightly built, Joan Rhodes retained her super-human strength until she died aged 89.

Revival (14): At the time of his death, Tommy Cooper was the latest in a long line of artistes who have died on stage, including Molière (1673), Sam Patch (1829), Kenneth Horne (1969). In 1984, the year Cooper died, Eric Morecambe suffered a fatal heart attack shortly after coming off stage following six curtain calls.

The Fish Fryer (15): One of Billy Bennet's catchphrases was, *If it's too big to shift, paint it!*

No Contest (16): Nervo and Knox were also members of the Crazy Gang, with Chesney Allen and Bud Flanagan.

Lady Be Good (17): During the heyday of Butlin's, Ivy Benson brought quality music to thousands of holidaymakers.

Hylda (18): Although essentially a live performer, Hylda Baker became known to millions, co-starring with Jimmy Jewel (with whom she had a fraught relationship) in the 1970s sitcom *Nearest and Dearest.*

Heart (20): Lottie Collins was enormously popular, and she made the song *Ta-ra-ra Boom-de-ay* into a national phenomenon. Many young men who idolised her were, shortly after her death, dying themselves in the trenches of World War I.

Glasgow Empire (21): When once asked on a radio quiz show, *Where did Napoleon die?* Eric Morecambe answered *The Glasgow Empire.*

Bad Impresario (24): The Palace, Halifax, where Baldwin's Catholic Geese received a standing ovation, is no longer with us but, in its heyday, it hosted four music hall shows a night. *Lady Clock-Eye* wished to be buried there, but isn't.

Accept No Imitations (23): In the asylum, J.D. Plummer was renowned for criticising his fellow inmates' basketwork.

Family Business (24): Jimmy Clitheroe launched his stage career because he was too small to work in the local weaving shed – he could not reach the looms.

My Old Man (25): Inspired by Ephraim, a small company in Lower Ecclestone provides a dad-o-gram service.

The Call of the Wild (26): In 2009 Sir David Attenborough hosted a BBC radio panel game, *The Percy Edwards Showdown*, dedicated to this extraordinary voice artist.

Raising Steam (28): After his train impersonation act, Reginald always finished with *Oh well, that's it, back to the asylum.*

And They're Off! (29): The comedian Jimmy James (see *Vintage*) began his stage career as one of Willy Netta's Singing Jockeys.

Night Class (30): Dick Emery became Chairman of the Airfix Appreciation Society.

The World's Greatest Whistler (31): At his peak, Ronnie Ronalde filled the Radio City Music Hall in New York (six thousand capacity) every night for ten weeks. His most famous hit was *If I Were a Blackbird.*

Morton Fraser's Harmaniacs (32): The dwarf was not only was not only an accomplished acrobat, but also a virtuoso harmonica and accordion player.

The Man with the Xylophone Skull (33): The term 'head banger' was coined to describe Professor Cheer's performance.

The Ray Conniff Singers (34): My family was subjected to this show at The Golden Garter, the most exclusive nightspot on Wythenshawe Council Estate.

Tiddly Om Pom Pom (36): Mark Sheridan wrote a serious role for himself as Napoleon in his musical burlesque *Gay Paree!*

Slave Song (37): Leslie Hutchinson, also known as Hutch, craved acceptance by upper-class society, which treated him dreadfully. He was adored by the masses.

Straight Man (38): The concept of comic and feed seems to be a more common characteristic of male double acts than female ones where the laugh-lines are often more evenly shared.

Frontiersman (39): After serving a particularly harsh prison sentence, *The Walsall Warrior* never performed again.

The Reluctant Sitter (40): This poem refers to this book's cover image, *Comedian's Corner*. Robert Rutherford was an entertainer, but it is Harry, his artist brother, who is featured in the painting. Many thanks are due to Robert's daughter Mary Fielder, executor of the estates of both brothers, for kindly giving permission for the painting to be reproduced on the cover.

Anthony Howell and His Disenchanted Pig (42): Anthony is a poet, former dancer with the Royal Ballet, tango teacher and performance artist. The pig spectacle was designed as a tribute to desire and cubism, but local dignitaries failed to appreciate its finer points.

Largesse (43): Teddy Brown argued he should get tax relief on the huge dinners he ate, because his size was an important part of his act. It went to court. He won.

The Art of Hunger (44): 'Fasting Men' were huge music hall attractions. Many, like Giovanni, were genuine. Kafka wrote a short story about one of them.

Praise Poem (45): Despite the fervour she attracted, Gracie Fields later also suffered vicious criticism for marrying an Italian during World War II.

Zazel, The Shooting Star! (46): The Great Farini was rivalled only by Blondin for his tightrope skills.

Without a Net (47): Selina Hunt was the first female tightrope artiste to become a national star.

Dr Zhivago (48): Robert Bolt, who wrote the screenplay, went to school with the uncle mentioned in this poem.

Power Sharing (49): Albert Black's wife called him Mr Lizard Hands because of how cold he could make his touch.

The Dancing Quakers (50): As a young man I occasionally attended Quaker meetings to catch up on some sleep.

Inextricable (51): J.H. Walter died homeless, with huge gambling debts, but his contortionist skills have been an inspiration to acrobats worldwide.

The Audience (52): Les Dawson's mother-in-law made him promise to never stop telling jokes about how awful she was. *Cosmo Smallpiece* was Les's inspired 'dirty old man' creation, using irony as criticism.

Exotica (54): Alejandra Dominquez made so much money, she retired at 30. Several politicians' wives tried to have her act banned.

Widow Twankey (55): Coincidentally, we have a male plumber in Halifax who goes about his business dressed as this famous panto character. He is a little expensive but worth it.

Burlington Bertie (56): Vesta Tilly remains the most famous male impersonator of all time. Rich young men would wear replicas of her suits.

Out from Under (57): Kate Cheval collapsed and died in the street, aged 15.

Mary Poppins (58): Testicular cancer is very rare in children. Dick Van Dyke's portrayal of a cockney chimney sweep can also cause grave discomfort.

Self Help (59): There has never been a more popular clown or panto performer than Joseph Grimaldi. In 1894 he played Dame Cicely Suet, the cook, in *Dick Whittington* at Drury Lane to three thousand people a night for three months.

Saddled (60): Harris Fitzpatrick was not the first pantomime horse, but he was the first to gain serious recognition. He coined the phrase, *You can take a horse to water but a pencil must be led.*

Better Out Than In (61): One of the stage personas George Formby Snr developed was that of John Willie, described by the historian Jeffrey Richards as the archetypal gormless Lancashire lad.

Beyond Belief (62): To combat the young Sid's stage fright, his mother Bertha would give him a glass of port before every performance. By the age of 13, Sid was dependent upon alcohol.

Crowd Control (63): Bigamy and incest were tolerated separately, but frowned upon when combined.

Engagement (64): During World War II, George Formby Jnr performed many times for troops on the front line, putting himself in great danger. ENSA – Entertainments National Service Association – was also called Every Night Something Awful.

Controlled Explosion (65): Edgar Kennedy was originally a light-heavyweight boxer. He went thirteen rounds with Jack Dempsey.

Le Pétomane (66): There are Neolithic stone engravings, thought by some to be carved in celebration of ancient flatulists.

Castrato (67): Handel was a great admirer of Farinelli who was not only one of the greatest opera singers of all time but also a harpsichordist and composer.

Tragedian (68): Burbage was Shakespeare's favourite tragedian. Off-stage he made a nuisance of himself as a practical joker.

Nightmare Scenario (69): Richard Dadd's paintings and pantomime backdrops have been exhibited in many premier galleries.

Lo! Hear the Gentle Lark (70): The same woman also performed an out-of-tune rendition of *Down Below*, a music hall song depicting the trials of being a sewage worker.

Foreign Exchange (71): Historically, only the Welsh and Scots have been more hated than the French by the English.

Counter Culture (72): Ted Olden later changed his name again, to Ted Ray, and became a household-name comedian who starred in his own show, *Ray's a Laugh!*

Brass Band (73): A friend of mine was told by his despairing trumpet teacher *You have an ear for music – Van Gogh's.*

Pleasure Craft (74): Russ Conway, diagnosed with stomach cancer in the late 1980s, founded the Russ Conway Cancer Fund and, despite failing health, performed many charity gala shows, raising thousands of pounds for cancer research.

Response (75): Joe Loss, despite a certain arrogance, was also a dedicated ENSA performer.

Bad Rap (76): As a boy, Leonard Norris showed great musical promise and was offered a scholarship but his parents prohibited him from accepting it.

Roughage (77): Omnivores – artistes who could eat anything – were a staple of music hall fare. A recent omnivore ate a whole Cessna light aircraft.

Three Sightings of Batman (78): Fathers For Justice campaigns for parliamentary support on issues such as custody of children and visiting rights.

The Hard Stuff (80): Buster Keaton's autobiography, *My Wonderful World of Slapstick*, is a work of profound wisdom. He is the only alcoholic I know of who cured himself without the help of any outside agencies.

Little Wonder (81): John Maskelyne wasn't the only artiste to expose spiritualists. Harry Houdini did too.

Go Gentle (82): Gilbert Harding concealed the fact that he was gay, which caused him deep unhappiness.

Street Cred (83): After years of struggle with drugs and alcohol, *Coronation Street* creator Tony Warren recovered to write several bestselling novels, one of the best being *The Lights of Manchester*.

The Man Who Killed Houdini (84): J. Gordon Whitehead was never convicted for Houdini's death, because Houdini invited the blow. Whitehead lived a troubled life and died a loner, an alcoholic, and a hoarder.

Here's Looking at You (85): A journalist with the *Illustrated London News* once asked Alice if she used hypnotism in her act. She simply stared at him. He broke down and had to leave the room.

Lament (86): *Sing Something Simple* was the longest-running BBC musical show ever.

Buccaneer (87): Jack Drake fathered four children, to different women, all members of the Pelican Players Amateur Operatic Society.

Double Act (88): Nicholas Parsons is the host of the long-running radio show *Just a Minute*. He has great legs.

Scandal (89): In 1938 Frank Randle formed his notorious touring troupe, *Randle's Scandals*.

Vintage (90): Another famous stage-drunk, Freddie Frinton, was also, like Jimmy James, a lifelong abstainer. The Germans watch Frinton's hilarious *Dinner for One* routine (see YouTube) every New Year.

Clever Bugger (91): Bob Monkhouse also wrote hundreds of sketches for many household-name comedians. He once had his joke book stolen, put out an appeal, and it was returned to him.

Civic Theatre (92): Amateur dramatics is currently enjoying a renaissance and is more popular than at any time since the 1940s. You have been warned.

Hostess Trolley (93): I am told that Geoffrey has now given up playing bowls, but he has never returned to the amateur stage.

Dumbing Up (94): There is, however, a terrific academic book, *The Golden Age of Pantomime*. See bibliography.

Town Crier (95): Shirley Bassey discouraged a move to make the song Diamonds Are Forever into a gay anthem.

Light Brigade (96): Lance Corporal Macauley would often quote Tennyson's words, *I must lose myself in action lest I wither in despair.*

Speech Coach (97): George Gorin was stabbed to death by a jealous lover of one his *Pedalling Princesses.*

A Funny Thing Happened… (98): Although Frankie Howerd's mannerisms appeared to be spontaneous, every pause, dither, stammer, tick, sigh were scripted and meticulously rehearsed. The poet Geoffrey Hill was a big fan.

Dun Roamin' (99): It is suggested that David Croft and Jimmy Perry modelled their *Dad's Army* character Captain Mainwaring on Gerald Butterworth, but I haven't been able to verify this.

Confidence Trick (100): When asked why he was so proud of his lack of talent, Bob Franklin answered, *It keeps me in touch with my public.*

Caretaker (101): Two other personnel at my secondary school were also rumoured to have had no toes: the metalwork teacher (it was thought an anvil had been dropped on his feet) and the deputy head teacher (cause unknown).

Immense (102): Little Tich – Harry Relph – actually invented the word *tich* (now *titch*). Facially, he resembled the Earl of Tichbourne. Along with Marie Lloyd and Dan Leno, Harry became the biggest music hall star both here and in Europe. You can still watch his 'big boot dance' on YouTube.

Above All (103): Later in his career, Clarence's act would cause him great discomfort and he would have to stay in bed for days after each performance: a very physical interpretation of the phrase *No pain, no gain.*

Vera (104): I last saw Vera working the phones in a taxi office.

Eleven, Plus (105): At the time of publication, Freddie Parrot-face Davies is alive and well. I had the honour of performing this sonnet for him at a recent comedy festival, and he kindly wrote *Bloody awful* on my copy.

Stepping Out (106): As well as footwear, Jack performed a vent act with a drunken doll, Willie Drinkall.

The Belly Dancers of Burnage (107): Burnage was described in an Anglo-Saxon document as *a place of evil wasteland.*

Crossing the Floor (108): The Tiller girls were formed in 1894. Betty Boothroyd, the former Speaker of the House of Commons, began her public career as a Tiller Girl.

The Highland Live-Wire (109): Although electroconvulsive therapy (ECT) is still administered, it is a highly controversial form of psychiatric treatment, and in many cases it has a damaging effect on brain tissue.

Hostilities (110): Lew Stone was also an accomplished pianist and arranger.

***I'm Here All Week*!** (112): I am told the full catchphrase is *I'm Here All Week Folks, Try The Veal!* I have no idea where this originated, or why.

All the Rage (113): St John's Ambulance Brigade volunteers attend many shows, hoping for something to do.

Chanteur (114): Jean Cocteau said *Before Charles Aznavour, despair was unpopular.*

Memory Man (116): Another music hall memory man was William Bottle, aka *Datas*. In the film *The Thirty-Nine Steps*, Wylie Watson played a character based on him.

Soul Mates (117): Throughout a lonely childhood, Arthur Rickett would invent many imaginary friends.

That's Your Lot (118): Tommy Cooper once said *If it wasn't for Tubby Turner, there'd be no Tommy Cooper*. This gives us an insight into Tubby's act.

Bibliography

Richard Baker, *British Music Hall* (Barnsley: Pen & Sword, 2014)

Richard Baker, *Old Time Variety* (Barnsley: Pen & Sword, 2011)

Louis Barfe, *Turned Out Nice Again* (London: Atlantic, 2008)

Freddie Davies, *Funny Bones* (Leeds: Scratching Shed, 2014)

Oliver Double, *Getting the Joke* (London: Bloomsbury Methuen, 2005)

Oliver Double, *Britain Had Talent* (Basingstoke: Palgrave Macmillan, 2012)

Tony Hannan: *On Behalf of the Committee* (Leeds: Scratching Shed, 2009)

Michael Kilgarrif: *Grace, Beauty & Banjos* (London: Oberon, 1999)

Sarah Maitland: *Vesta Tilly* (London: Virago 1988)

John Major. *My Old Man* (London: Harper Collins, 2012)

Andy Merriman: *Greasepaint & Cordite* (London: Aurum, 2013)

Eric Midwinter: *Make 'Em Laugh* (London: Allen & Unwin, 1979)

Bob Monkhouse: *Crying with Laughter* (London: Arrow, 1993)

Jeffrey Richards: *The Golden Age of Pantomime* (London: Taurus, 2015)